Violin 2

FOLK SONGS of AUSTRALIA

STRINGS AROUND THE WORLD

for String Orchestra or String Quartet
Arranged by LOIS SHEPHEARD

Violin 1

Violin 2

Viola

Cello

String Bass

Violin 3 (Viola t.c.)

Piano Accompaniment

CONTENTS

Barn Dance, *Australian Folk Song* 7

The Black Velvet Band, *Australian Folk Song* 8

Botany Bay, *Australian Folk Song* 9

Brisbane Ladies, *Australian Folk Song* 10

Click Go the Shears, *Australian Folk Song* 11

Jim Jones at Botany Bay, *Australian Folk Song* 12

Kookaburra, *Sinclair* 13

Along the Road to Gundagai, *O'Hagan* 14

A Thousand Miles Away, *Australian Folk Song* 14

Waltzing Matilda, *Cowan* 15

Art Layout: LISA GREENE MANE

© 1999 Summy-Birchard Music
division of Summy-Birchard Inc.
All Rights Reserved   Printed in USA

Summy-Birchard Inc.
exclusively distributed by
Warner Bros. Publications
15800 NW 48th Avenue
Miami, Florida 33014

ISBN 0-87487-784-9

Any duplication, adaptation or arrangement of the compositions
contained in this collection requires the written consent of the Publisher.
No part of this book may be photocopied or reproduced in any way without permission.
Unauthorized uses are an infringement of the U.S. Copyright Act and are punishable by law.

INTRODUCTION

This collection of tuneful Australian music is designed for the student string orchestra. The arrangements often take the tunes a step further than their original musical intention, but they are not technically difficult. There is a 3rd violin part matching the viola part, and the violin teacher with no access to viola, cello or bass students will find that the piano part provides an alternative.

If using these pieces for string quartet, please note that "Barn Dance" and "Kookaburra" require the cellist to play the cued double bass notes.

THE SONGS

Convicts from England first settled Australia and they, together with free settlers, began to provide us with folk music. The tunes were often adapted from folk songs of the British Isles. The ballads depict various aspects of early Australian history.

Songs mentioning "Botany Bay" (penal settlement) tell of the sadness of being transported from England and of the brutal conditions aboard convict ships. Similarly, "The Black Velvet Band" is the ballad of an Irishman tricked by a girl wearing a black velvet hair-band. He was found guilty of the robbery she had committed and sent to Van Dieman's Land (now Tasmania).

Those men who mustered and drove cattle across this enormous country provided us with songs such as "Brisbane Ladies," the girls on Queensland cattle stations who enjoyed dancing waltzes and polkas with the rovers. The sheep industry is represented by "Click Go the Shears." Early history of the meat industry using transport by Cobb and Co.'s horse-drawn carriages and the earliest railways is described in "A Thousand Miles Away."

"Gundagai" is a town in a pastoral area of New South Wales; the "Barn Dance" is self-explanatory. "Kookaburra" is our beloved bird of the Kingfisher family with a call resembling a human laugh. The well-known "Waltzing Matilda" is a tale of a bushman carrying his belongings rolled up in his blanket (his matilda).

Lois Shepheard

INTRODUCCIÓN

Esta colección de melodiosa música australiana está diseñada para orquestas de cuerdas de estudiantes. Frecuentemente, los arreglos llevan las melodías un paso más allá de su intención musical original, pero no son técnicamente difíciles. Se incluye una 3ª parte de violín armonizada a la par de la de viola, y el maestro de violín que no tenga estudiantes de viola, violoncelo o contrabajo notará que la parte de piano proporciona una alternativa.

Al usar estas piezas para cuarteto de cuerdas, es necesario notar que "Barn Dance" y "Kookaburra" requieren que el violoncelista toque las notas del contrabajo denotadas en tamaño pequeño.

LAS CANCIONES

Los convictos ingleses fueron los primeros en establecerse en Australia, y conjuntamente con colonos libres, empezaron a proporcionarnos música folklórica. Las canciones eran a menudo adaptaciones de canciones folklóricas de las islas británicas. Las baladas describen varios aspectos de historia temprana australiana.

Las canciones que mencionan a "Botany Bay" (colonia penal) describen la tristeza de ser transportado desde Inglaterra, y de las condiciones brutales a bordo de los navios de convictos. De la misma forma, "The Black Velvet Band" es la balada de un irlandés, engañado por una muchacha que se sujetaba el cabello con una banda de terciopelo negro. Fue declarado culpable por un robo que ella cometió, y fue enviado a la tierra de Dieman (en el presente, Tasmania).

Esos hombres que briosamente guiaban el ganado a través de este enorme país nos han dado canciones como "Brisbane Ladies, "— las muchachas de las estaciones de ganado en Queensland, que disfrutaban al bailar valses y polcas con los arrieros. La industria ovejera es representada por "Click Go the Shears." La canción "A Thousand Miles Away" describe los comienzos de la historia de la industria ganadera y el transporte del ganado en los carruajes tirados por caballos de Cobb y Co, y los primeros ferrocarriles.

"Gundagai" es un pueblo de la zona pastoril de Nueva Gales Sur; "Barn Dance" se explica por sí misma. "Kookaburra" es nuestro amado pájaro de la familia del martín pescador, con un canto parecido a la risa humana. La muy conocida canción "Waltzing Matilda" relata la historia de un aborigen que lleva sus pertenencias enrolladas en su manta (su matilda).

Lois Shepheard

INTRODUCTION

Cette colléction de musiques harmonieuses Australiennes est destinée aux étudiants d'instruments à cordes. Très souvent les arrangements prennent un air un pas plus loin de leur intention musicale originale, mais ils ne sont pas compliqués. Il y a un troisième rôle de violon qui accompagne le rôle de l'alto, et le professeur de violon qui n'a pas d'accès à l'alto et les éudiants de violoncelle ou de basse, trouveront que le rôle du piano offre une alternative.

Quand ces pièces sont utilisées pour un quatuor à cordes, vous noterez que le "Barn Dance" et le "Kookaburra" exigent que le violoncelliste execute les notes d'entrée en contrebasse.

LES CHANSONS

Au début les condamnés en provenance d'Angleterre s'établirent en Australie et, ensemble avec les colons libres, ils commencèrent à nous fournir de la musique folklorique. Très souvent les mélodies dérivent de chansons folkloriques provenant des Iles Britanniques. Les ballades décrivent les divers aspects de l'ancienne histoire Australienne.

Les chansons qui mentionnent le "Botany Bay" (une colonie pénitentiaire) parlent de la tristesse d'être déportés d'Angleterre et des conditions sauvages à bord des navires de condamnés. De même, "The Black Velvet Band" est la ballade d'un Irlandais trompé par une femme portant un bandeau de velours noir. Il avait été reconnu coupable d'un vol qu'elle avait commis et envoyé à Van Demian (aujourd'hui la Tasmanie).

Ces hommes qui groupaient et conduisaient le bétail à travers cet énorme pays, nous ont fourni de chansons telles que "Brisbane Ladies," les jeunes femmes des stations de bétail à Queensland qui s'amusaient à dancer les valses et les polkas avec eux. L'industrie de la laine est representée par "Click Go the Shears." La "A Thousand Miles Away" parle de l'ancienne histoire de l'elevage bovin qui utilisait, comme méthode de transport les voitures de la Cobb and Co. traînées par des chevaux et l'ancien chemin de fer.

"Gundagai" est un village situé dans une région champêtre du Nouveau Galles du Sud; la "Barn Dance" s'explique de soi-même. "Kookaburra" est notre oiseau chéri de la famille du Martin-pêcheur dont le cri ressemble au rire humain. La fameuse "Walzing Matilda" est l'histoire d'un Boschiman transportant ses objets personnels roulés dans sa couverture (sa Matilda).

Lois Shepheard

EINFÜHRUNG

Diese Sammlung melodischer Australischer Musik wurde für Schüler Streichorchester zusammengestellt. Die Arrangements gehen über die originale musikalische Absicht etwas hinaus, aber sie sind vom Technischen her nicht schwierig. Es gibt eine dritte Geigenstimme die zu der der Viola paßt. Sollte der Geigenlehrer nicht über einen Violapart verfügen, bietet der Klavier Part den Cello- und Baß-Schülern eine Alternative.

Falls Sie diese Stücke für ein Streichquartet benutzen wollen, beachten Sie bitte daß für die Stücke ‚Barn Dance' und ‚Kookaburra' ein Cellist erforderlich wird, um die Doppelbaß Noten zu spielen.

ÜBER DIESE LIEDER

Häftlinge von England waren die ersten Siedler in Australien. Sie brachten uns zusammen mit freien Siedlern, die erste Volksmusik. Die Lieder waren often den Volksliedern der Britischen Inseln nachempfunden. Die Balladen beschreiben verschiedene Aspekte der frühen Australischen Geschichte.

Es gibt Lieder die ‚Botany Bay' erwähnen. Dies war eine Sträflingslager und die Lieder berichten von der Trauer über den Verlust des Heimatlandes und den brutalen Lebensbedingungen an Bord der Sträflingsschiffe. In ähnlicher Weise ist ‚The Black Velvet Band' die Ballade eines Irländers, der von einem Mädchen mit einem schwarzen Samt-Haarband hereingelegt wurde. Er wurde eines Raubüberfalles für schuldig befunden, den das Mädchen begangen hatte, und wurde zum Van Dieman`s Land geschickt. (Das heutige Tasmanien)

Männern, die Rinder züchteten und durch dieses riesige Land trieben, haben wir Lieder zu verdanken wie ‚Brisbane Ladies', das sind die jungen Damen in Queensland Rinder-Stationen, die gerne Polkas und Walzer mit den Rindertreibern tanzten. Die Schafzucht ist durch das Lied ‚Click Go the Shears' repräsentiert. In dem Lied ‚A Thousand Miles Away' wird die frühe Geschichte der Fleischerei-Industrie beschrieben, die zum Transport die Pferdewagen der Firma Cobb & Co. und die ersten Bahnverbindungen benutzten.

‚Gundagai' ist ein Ort in einer ländlichen Gegend von New South Wales; der ‚Barn Dance' (Scheunentanz) erklärt sich von selbst. ‚Kookaburra' ist ein beliebter Vogel aus der Familie der Königsfischer, dessen Ruf dem Lachen eines Menschen ähnlich ist. Das bekannte Lied der ‚Waltzing Matilda' ist die Geschichte eines Buschmannes, der seine Habe in eine Decke aufgerollt mit sich trägt (seine Matilda).

Lois Shepheard

INTRODUZIONE

Questa collezione di musica armoniosa Australiana é destinata a studenti di strumenti a corda. Gli arrangiamenti spesso prendono toni un passo oltre la loro originale intenzione musicale, ma non sono tecnicamente difficili. C'é una terza parte da violino che accompagna la viola. Il maestro di violino, che non ha accesso ad una viola, e gli studenti di violoncello o basso, troveranno che la parte del piano provvede un'alternativa.

Nel caso in cui questi pezzi vengano utilizzati per quartetto d'archi, dovrà essere preso nota che "Barn Dance" e "Kookaburra" richiede che il suonatore di violoncello esegua le note di attacco in contrabbasso.

LE CANZONI

I condannati provenienti dall'Inghilterra prima colonizzarono l'Australia ed insieme ai liberi coloni, iniziarono a fornirci la musica folcloristica. Spesso, le melodie derivavano da canzoni popolari provenienti dalle Isole Britanniche. Le ballate dipingono variati aspetti della remota storia Australiana.

Le canzoni che menzionano "Botany Bay" (una colonizzazione penale) raccontano della tristezza dell'essere deportati dall'Inghilterra e delle brutali condizioni a bordo delle navi galeotte. Similarmente, "The Black Velvet Band" é la ballata di uno Scozzese ingannato da una donna con un turbante di velluto nero. Fu giudicato colpevole di un furto da lei commesso e spedito nella terra di Van Demian (oggi la Tasmania).

Quegli uomini che adunavano e conducevano il bestiame attraverso questo enorme paese ci hanno fornito canzoni quali "Brisbane Ladies" le giovani donne nelle stazioni di bestiame che amavano ballare il valzer e la polka con i mandriani. L'industria ovina viene rappresentata da "Click Go the Shears." Nella "A Thousand Miles Away" viene descritta la remota storia dell'industria bovina usante carrozze trainate da cavalli e le primitive ferrovie della Cobb e Co.

"Gundagai" é una cittadina in una zona pastorale nel Nuovo Galles del Sud; la "Barn Dance" é autoesplicativo. "Kookaburra" é il nostro amato uccello della famiglia del martin pescatore con il richiamo simile ad una risata umana. La famosa "Walzing Matilda" e' la novella di un Boshimano che trasporta i suoi averi arrotolati nella sua coperta (la sua Matilda).

Lois Shepheard

INTRODUÇÃO

Esta coleção de melodiosas canções Australianas foi especialmente desenvolvida para o estudante de orquestra de cordas. As mesmas foram arranjadas de forma que o aluno se indentifique com os temas e não se amendronte com o nível de dificuldade por elas exigida. A partitura assinalada ao terceiro violino é a mesma da viola. Professores de violino que não tem acesso a estudantes de viola, violoncelo ou contrabaixo encontrarão as partituras para o piano como alternativa.

Ao utilizar estas composições para quarteto de cordas, prestar atenção que as canções "Barn Dance" e "Kookaburra" requerem que o violoncelista participe em específicas partes assinaladas ao contra-baixo.

AS CANÇÕES

Presos convictos e colonos Ingleses começaram a compôr os primórdios do folclore Australiano. A música se baseava, e muitas vezes era adaptada, nas canções folclóricas das Ilhas Britânicas. As baladas descrevem muitos aspectos do início da história da Austrália.

Em algumas canções observa-se um sentimento de penúria devido a árdua viagem de transferência dos presos convictos à Austrália, exemplo claro disso apresenta-se na canção de título "Botany Bay" que significa punição penal severa. Simirlamente, a canção "The Black Velvet Band" tem como tema a traição de uma mulher, que acusou seu próprio amante de cometer um crime que ela mesmo havia cometido. O pobre homem foi julgado e condenado a prisão perpétua na cadeia da Ilha de Van Dieman, mais conhecida atualmente como Tasmânia.

Os temas do faroeste e cowboys cruzando as imensas planícies da Austrália nos trouxeram canções como "Brisbane Ladies" (As Mulheres de Brisbane), que conta a história das mulheres que esperavam os cowboys nas feiras agropecuária e se divertiam dançando valsas e polkas até o amanhecer. Os criadores de ovelha também contam suas estórias na canção "Click Go the Shears" (Amolem suas Tesouras). O início da história da indústria bovina é descrito na canção "A Thousand Miles Away" (Mil Milhas Distante), que fala sobre as carroças da companhia Cobb & Co. e das antigas locomotivas responsáveis pelo transporte da carne durante esse período.

"Gundagai" é uma cidade localizada na área pastoreira de New South Wales, um dos estados Australianos; a canção "Barn Dance" (Dança do Celeiro) nem necessita explicação. "Kookaburra" é o papagaio que ria como gente de verdade e pertencia a família Kingfisher. A famosa "Waltzing Matilda" fala da lenda de um andarilho que carregava todos os seus pertences enrolados num cobertor que ele chamava Matilda.

Lois Shepheard

BARN DANCE

Australian Folk Tune
Arranged by LOIS SHEPHEARD

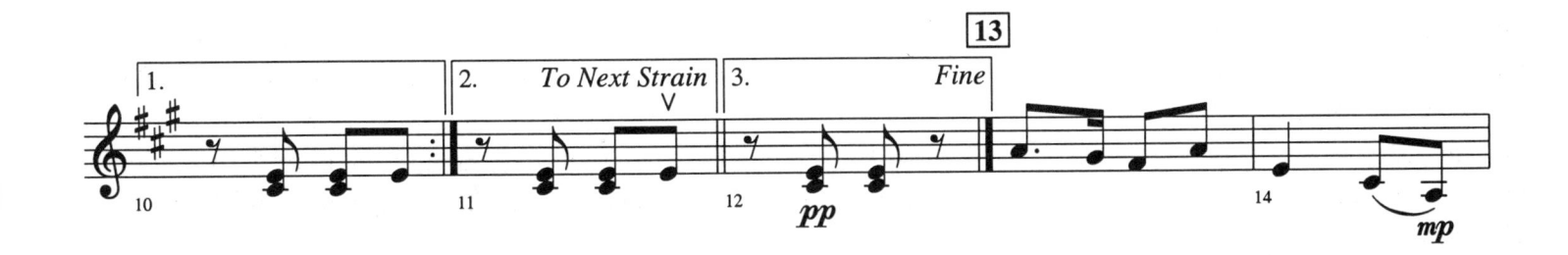

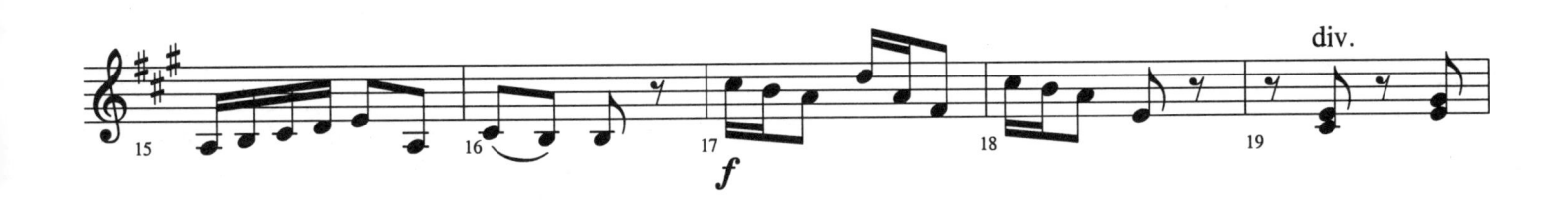

VIOLIN 2

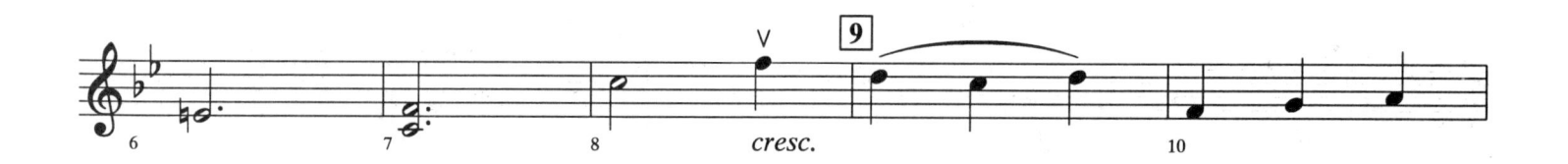

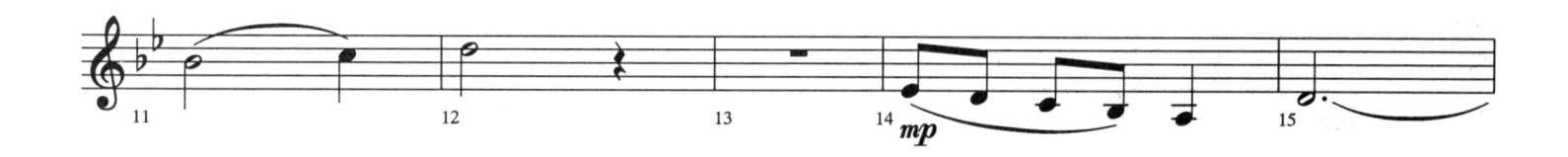

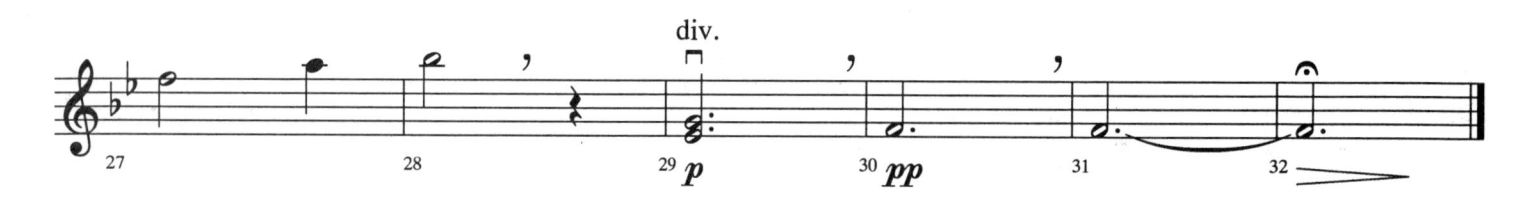

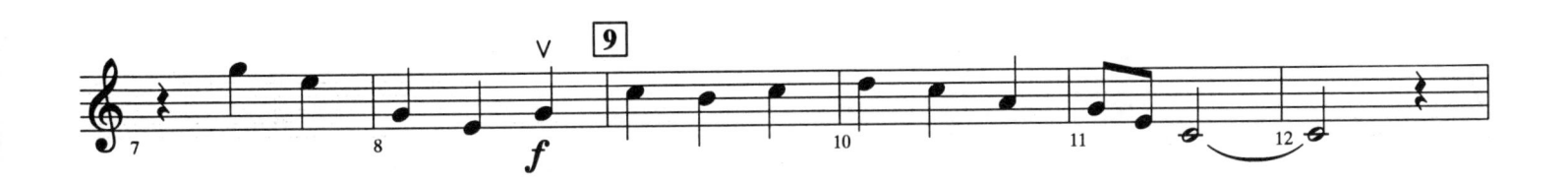

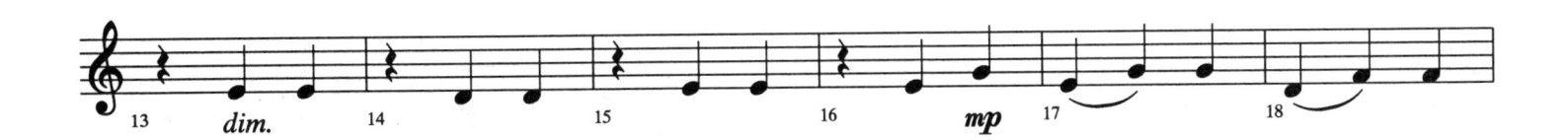

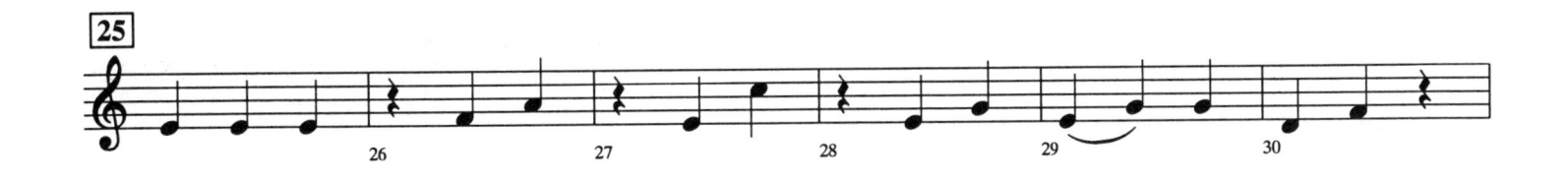

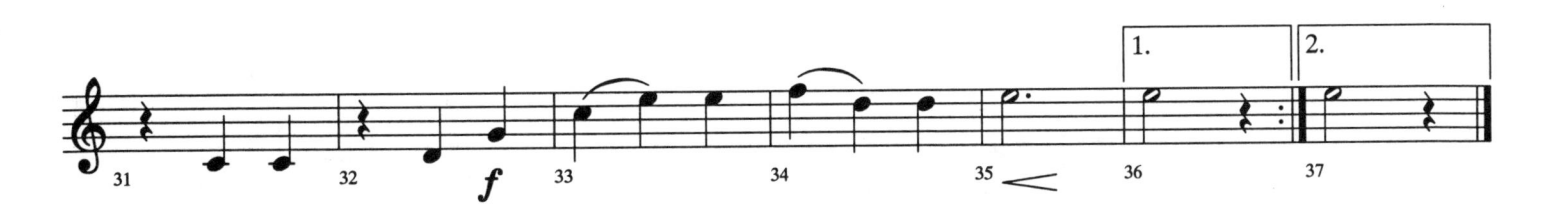

BRISBANE LADIES

Australian Folk Tune
Arranged by LOIS SHEPHEARD

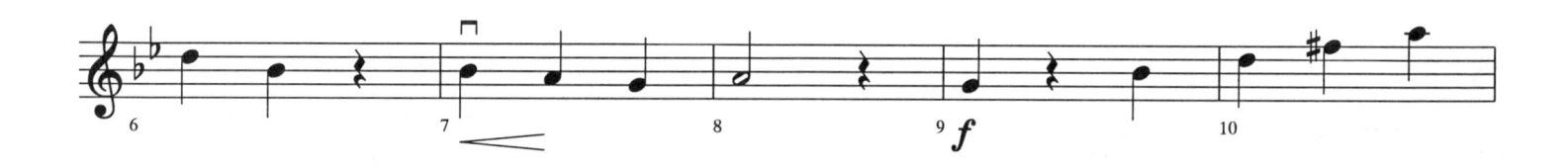

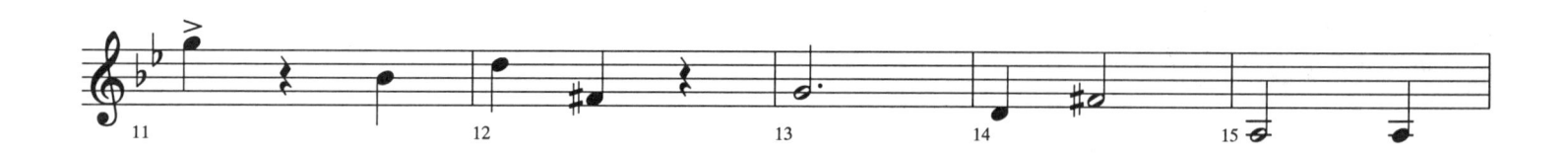

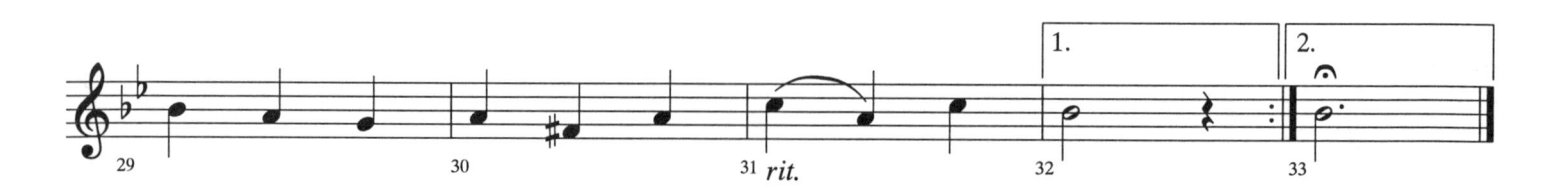

CLICK GO THE SHEARS

VIOLIN 2

Australian Folk Tune
Arranged by LOIS SHEPHEARD

JIM JONES AT BOTANY BAY

Australian Folk Tune
Arranged by LOIS SHEPHEARD

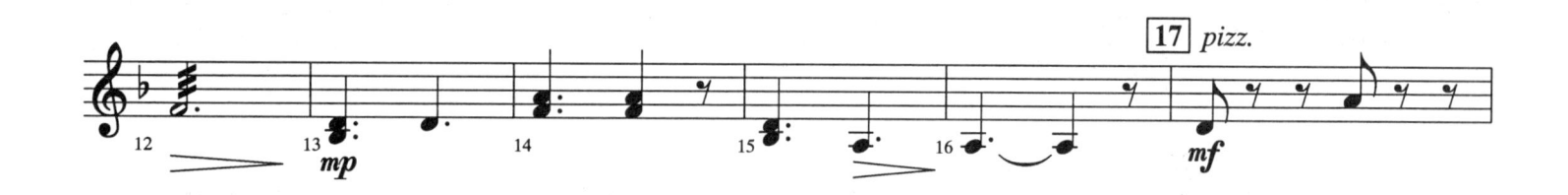

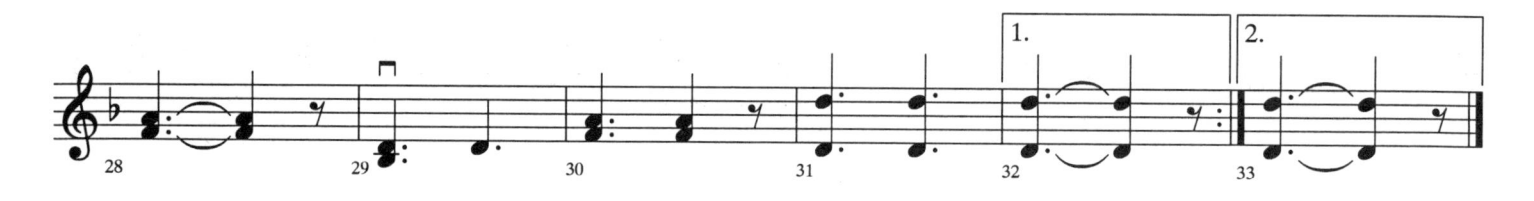

KOOKABURRA

ALONG THE ROAD TO GUNDAGAI

O'Hagan
Arranged by LOIS SHEPHEARD

VIOLIN 2

A THOUSAND MILES AWAY

Australian Folk Tune
Arranged by LOIS SHEPHEARD

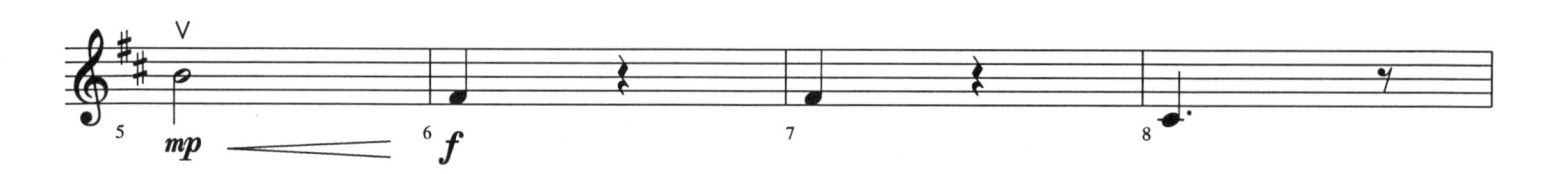

VIOLIN 2

© 1999 Summy-Birchard Music
division of Summy-Birchard Inc.
exclusively distributed by Warner Bros. Publications
15800 NW 48th Avenue Miami, Florida 33014
All rights reserved   Printed in USA

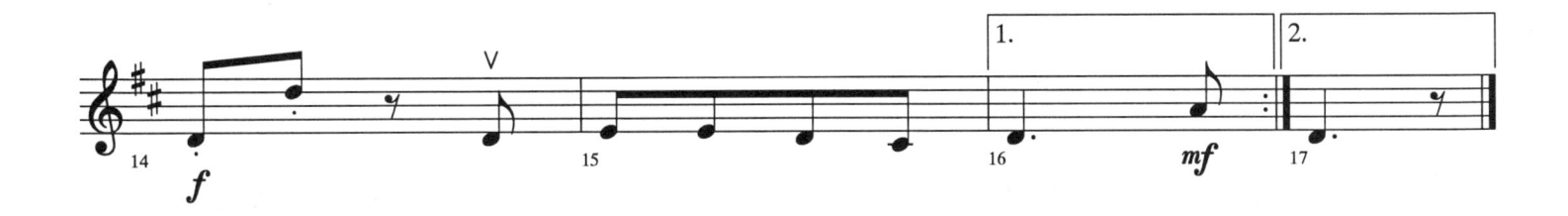

WALTZING MATILDA

Cowan
Arranged by LOIS SHEPHEARD

VIOLIN 2

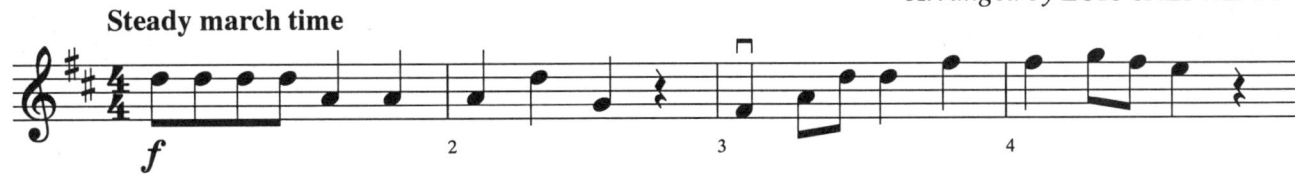